THE T.E.A.M.

TALENTED EMPOWERED ASPIRED MEN

Character & Integrity of Manhood

By
Casey Chinedu Ifedi & Chris Graham

The T.E.A.M:
Character & Integrity of Manhood

Published by Victorious You Press™

Copyright © 2020 by Casey Chinedu Ifedi & Chris Graham

All rights reserved.

No part of this book may be reproduced, distributed or transmitted in any form by any means, graphic, electronic, or mechanical, including photocopy, recording, taping, or by any information storage or retrieval system, without permission in writing from the author except in the case of reprints in the context of reviews, quotes, or references.

Unless otherwise indicated, scripture quotations are from the Holy Bible, New King James Version. All rights reserved.

Printed in the United States of America

ISBN: 978-1-952756-10-8

For details email vyp.joantrandall@gmail.com
or visit us at www.victoriousyoupress.com

Dedication

Dedication and thanks go to the authors and collaborators of this book. I dedicate this book to everyone that has contributed to make this manhood movement possible. To you the reader, thank you for taking the time to learn about the true essence of manhood and what is needed of men of today.

This book is dedicated to the true internal man that lives deep inside: to purpose, true manhood, self-love, and divine direction. All praises to The Most High God. I dedicate this work to you. To every man and woman that loves Him and wants to learn more about real, authentic manhood, I dedicate the golden standard of manhood in the 21st century to you.

With love and care,

Acknowledgement

We are truly blessed by so many people who played a part to make this book a reality and had a major impact on the success of *T.E.A.M.* If we tried to name them all, we are worried that someone might be left out. Please know that we are extremely fortunate to have so many great friends. We want to thank the men who dedicated their time in each chapter to share their amazing stories. Your kind words of wisdom, knowledge, and empowerment will enrich many lives present and in the future.

We deeply appreciate the motivation and spiritual dedication from Joan Randall to bring our vision to reality. We are thankful for her friendship—a friendship filled with deep and transparent conversation. The longer we share the air, the better I feel the breeze of love and family on my soul.

Foreword

The construct of this book is about the journey to manhood. Although each story is unique, it will address how men have navigated the obstacle course of life to become a man. In today's society, men are challenged and prone to face a myriad of adversities. However, character and integrity must be the hallmark of true manhood. Men must be unified in their effort to seek positive change while realizing perseverance and persistence are paramount to their growth.

By today's standards, black males are living in turbulent times. "Historically, racism and discrimination have inflicted a variety of harsh injustices on African Americans in the United States, especially on males. Being male and black has meant being psychologically castrated—rendered impotent in the economic, political, and social arenas that whites have 'historically' dominated." [1] In many instances, their plight externally

---

[1] Richard Majors and Janet Mancini Billson, *Cool Pose* "Expressions and Survival." (New York: Lexington Books, 1992)

reflects a perception of a lack of character and integrity.

Internally, as men we must find common ground as a T.E.A.M. to motivate and encourage each other. We must strive toward a common purpose…to establish a burning desire to succeed. My prescription for manhood, in accordance with many of the comments in this book, is God, myself, family, my profession, and my community. I believe we are all called to serve.

This book represents a blueprint that expresses many ideas about character, integrity, and manhood. It provides various elements of insight through commentary by a variety of contributors. This manuscript provides diverse strategies elaborated on from a variety of personal experiences. Everyone has a story. In many cases—they have similarities.

Commonalities of this book suggest that we should never relinquish our character and integrity, which is a moral imperative. In addition, an important factor of manhood is that we can never become complacent. I commend this manuscript for all men and others that seek to gain knowledge and insight, which will foster and perpetuate high character with integrity.

— *George F. Spencer*

CONTENTS

Dedication i

Acknowledgement iii

Foreword v

Introduction 1

Be a Victim or a Change Agent: *By Henry (Hank) R. Fore* 3

Be Present and Have a Presence: *By Carlas (CJ) Quinney* 11

Getting Back in The Fight: *By Mike Sexton* 19

Integrity in The New Millennium: *By Kendall Taylor* 27

Generational Man: *By Chris Graham* 37

Success Driven: *By Jervay Vanderhorst* 45

Character and the Integrity of a Man: *By Peter Adamson* 51

Leverage: *By Harold Sendar* 59

GROWN Man: *By Dr. Lathan Turner* 69

Trophies *What* "Making It Look Easy" Means and Why It Is Important as Men: *By Jamine C. Ifedi, MBA* 79

Men of T.E.A.M.: *By Casey C. Ifedi* 89

About The Authors 99

INTRODUCTION

---⋙◦◦⋘---

How would you complete this sentence? Character and integrity of manhood is...

Think about it. What words or thoughts run across your mind? Somewhere, you learned the image of manhood. Someone may have told you. Character and integrity men are in charge, never cry, get all of the women, and are always right. These types of messages run across our society. The stereotype of the tough guy with strong arms permeates catalogs and cartoons. But are they the measures of manhood? Is character and integrity defined by dumbbell lifting and female conquering? If so, most of us guys fail the manhood test. Truth is, not all of us lift weights or lead groups.

Some of us shed tears, walk briskly, and get downright nervous talking to ladies. There must be more to understanding character and integrity of manhood than what we learn in the locker room. Surely there is. The dream for men in God's eyes includes words of eternal consequence. Words like: *humble*, *loyal*, *father*, *joy*, *prayer*, and *purpose*. God has equipped you with the ability to desire to love, forgive, dream, to fulfill, and most of all, share amongst others. Men with character and integrity pray, cherish their wives and love their children, and open up to friends.

Men with character and integrity are a T.E.A.M. (Talented Empowered Aspired Men).

If such an image intrigues you, then you are holding the right book. You have in your hands the collaboration of eleven men sharing their personal growth from adolescence to manhood, while exploring how they understand character and integrity, and how it is important for the 21st century man. You will be encouraged, impacted, and uplifted by these stories. You will learn how to implement these practical principles into your life. Interested? Then turn the page. Men with character and integrity want to improve their manhood.

BE A VICTIM OR A CHANGE AGENT

By Henry (Hank) R. Fore

We all have a story. Mine may be similar to others that you know, and perhaps you can relate to it. I grew up in a small town north of Pittsburgh, Pennsylvania. My father worked in a steel mill and served as a part-time pastor at a local church. Mom was a housewife who raised five children—three boys and two girls—and I was the oldest.

My early years were that of a normal young man. I did well academically in school, took part in sports, and loved everything outdoors like camping, hunting, and fishing. Church and faith were important. I had a few close friends. My big dream was to fly jets in the Air Force.

Life was good until the ninth grade. My father was an alcoholic. He eventually spent time in the State Hospital and received shock treatments. His disease progressed to the point that he became so physically abusive to my mother that I had to intervene many times to protect her from harm. He eventually burned down our home and abandoned our family. We lost everything. I was fifteen years old.

Goodbye adolescence. This is when and why I became the man I am today. I had two options: be a *Victim* or become a *Change Agent*.

It's no surprise that this traumatic event created a family of victims. *Victims* sometimes acquiesce to self-pity and a "woe is me" attitude. They often succumb to depression and give up on life, family, friends, and themselves. Victims of these types of situations seek others to console them, which we did. The embarrassment and grief were overwhelming. It would have been easy for me to let the hatred for my father bring me down and run from it all. As a single parent of five children, my mother also faced hard decisions.

In difficult circumstances, some people choose to become a *Change Agent*. Adversity is often the opportunity that drives positive changes in our lives. Let it motivate you to change your current situation. That's what I did. I manned up. I was not wired to have people feel sorry for me, and neither was my mother.

As the oldest, I let the hurt motivate me to help my mother and siblings survive. Even though we had initial support from our local family and church, it fell upon me to work with my mom to raise my four younger siblings. I was only in high school and had to balance studies, sports, and multiple part-time jobs to ensure we were clothed and fed.

This experience was the best opportunity that happened in my life to mold my character. I was a young teenager thrust into a world that required me to suddenly become an adult. I quickly learned the importance of discipline, focus, work ethics, respect for others, integrity, and courage. More importantly, I had to become a role model for my siblings. To encourage them I said, "Don't give up moving forward or give in to the victim attitude. We still need an education and to support each other."

Mom and I worked at Perkins Pancake House Restaurant in Hickory, Pennsylvania. I was a short order cook and she was the restaurant's prep cook. We commuted back and forth together on the weekends and some evenings. Those were precious moments. We talked about the restaurant staff, how tired we were of smelling like pancake batter and grease, and just life in general.

I learned early on that family was the most important priority, regardless of your age and circumstance. I understood the value of hard work. I washed cars, cut lawns, babysat, life guarded, and performed any job to help the family.

Again, I could have taken the *Victim* attitude route and let my grades slip while working all the jobs—but I didn't. At the age of eight, I clearly knew what I wanted to do in life. I held onto those goals and dreams. I studied harder…and worked even harder. I was going to be the *Agent of Change* in our family and the first to attend college. I dealt with the adversity. I was not perfect and made mistakes but stayed the course.

I eventually graduated high school with honors and voted "Most Likely to Succeed." I turned down an appointment to the United States Air Force Academy because they would not let me fly jets—their loss. I did graduate from the United States Military Academy at West Point and served twenty-four years in the United States Army retiring as a Lieutenant Colonel. I spent another twenty years in the private sector and successfully ran businesses in start-up companies up to a $5 billion business in a Fortune 50 corporation. I am grateful for the great successes, rewards, and recognition over several careers. Not bad for a boy from the projects.

The military and the private sector both supplied challenges that required me to reach deep inside at times and occasionally test my resolve. I would always reflect on my past. My single mother raised five children. I would tell myself, "Stop feeling sorry for yourself and get on with it! Welcome to manhood."

Manhood is that transition from dependency to being independent. It's the ability to make your own decisions and think for yourself. You create your own value system and live by it. It's knowing right from wrong, and more importantly, doing what is right for the right reason.

Manhood is a State of Mind. It encompasses Courage, Confidence, Compassion, and Humility. Hard work is your battle cry because nothing is free, and do not expect it. Old School says you need to earn your success honestly. Respect your family and women. That's manhood!

Here are a few mantras that I've carried through life because of my early life experiences. They may be useful for any man or woman in today's world.

1. Failure is not an option. My siblings and mother had to survive. I use this slogan as the foundation in every task I take on in life. Yes, I've failed or disappointed many times, but I always try something new and never give up. I believe in the 90/10 rule. You'll get it right 90% of the time and fail 10%. The most important principle is that you do not give up on the 10%. Keep working at it or trying something different. Take some calculated risks. You will eventually succeed.

2. 100/0. This is a principle I saw on a TED Talk many years ago. Leadership expert Dr. John Izzo's basic message was to take 100% Responsibility/Accountability and Zero Excuses. This simple idea resonated with me so much that I created this as a rally cry in several of my businesses. Again, it's easier to submit to failure or become a victim. I argue it's harder to take 100% responsibility for your actions and not make excuses. Go out and fix it. Change the world.

3. Protect your character. Your character boils down to *what you do when no one is looking*. The essence of your character is the values, integrity, courage, passion, and humility you exude each day of your life. Others will judge you on these attributes. My character was molded early in life, and I protect it at all costs.

A test of that character was the courage I exhibited when I finally forgave my father right before he passed away in 2013. My faith told me it was the right action to take for the right reason.

Finally, my mother was the most wonderful, strongest woman I've known in my life. She was my role model and mentor. She passed away too young in May 2007 to cancer. She had only a third-grade education. I always remember her one wish. "I want all my children to graduate high school."

Well, all five of us graduated high school, and we achieved much more. We embraced change in the face of tragedy. Failure was not an option!

T.E.A.M. Manhood Golden Standard: Take 100% Responsibility/Accountability and Zero Excuses. Believe in the 90/10 rule. You'll get it right 90% of the time and fail 10%. The most important principle is that you do not give up on the 10%. Keep working at it or trying something different. Take some calculated risks. You will eventually succeed. Your character boils down to *what you do when no one is looking*. The essence of your character is the values, integrity, courage, passion, and humility you exude each day of your life.

BE PRESENT AND HAVE A PRESENCE

By Carlas (CJ) Quinney

To me, especially growing up black, my dad was the example of what a perfect father was. What I mean about *perfect* is…he did not do everything perfect, but he had perfect intentions. Whether you are a father or not, the question I have is, "Are you present?"

Growing up, my dad was present. I found out young that not only was I lucky to have a father but one who was present. I remember in elementary school my dad would drive on all the field trips. Even though other parents had their vehicles, all my classmates said, "We want to ride with Mr. Quinney!" As a child, I never understood why they wanted to ride with my dad…I sure didn't. I tried to ride with the other parents. My classmates fought over the seats to ride with my dad. It was not until I was older that I realized they were attracted to my father because they did not have one. So, to me the integrity of a man, husband, or father is being present.

The second question I have about character and integrity is, "Are you showing up?" Not just being present, but do you have a presence? The number one quality my dad taught me is "Are you a man of your word?"

I have a homie named Marcus, and what's funny is we recently did a podcast with him. He has two successful restaurants in Houston, and he said, "The key to excellence for me is we open when we say we are going to open, and everything we have on the menu is available." I look at fatherhood, manhood, character, and integrity the same way. It is not that complex. Can you be present, can you have a presence, and can you do what you say you are going to do?

I remember my friend's father would say, "I am going to take you to laser tag," and he would never show up. He just did not have any integrity.

My third question is, "Can you do what you say you are going to do?" Are you a man of your word? You can get to the point where you keep your word, and people can have a lot of respect for you. If I tell you, "I am going to show up Friday at eleven o'clock," unless there is an emergency, I will be there. This seems like a simple task, but it is actually hard for a lot of men because they choose not to keep their word.

I was maturing from adolescence to manhood when I realized that life was not just about me. I have a six-year-old and a three-year-old, and they fight over toys. Their actions are not about me. When I was fifteen or sixteen years old, I started to feel that I had an obligation to *do for others*. I heard this when I was young, but it just didn't click how important it was to help others as part of manhood.

When I turned seventeen, I decided to volunteer for the Big Brothers and Big Sisters program. I felt grateful to be able to play ball, live the middle-class lifestyle, and have my father in my life. I thought, "Damn, I am lucky to have a pops." Most of my friends did not have their pops around, and I felt growing up from adolescence to manhood meant to give back. So, I went to Big Brothers and Big Sisters and asked to become a mentor. They said, "You are not old enough." I felt disappointed but did not give up.

The summer I was eighteen, I went back and started mentoring a young man. I began to see him thrive and thought, "I was put on this earth to do more than just for myself." That was the moment I saw my transition from adolescence to manhood.

I think we need more good examples of manhood. That is why I appreciate men like LeBron James. He put a social media post of his kids dancing. I sent it to my boy and said, "He doesn't have to do that." You LeBron! He has a net worth close to a billion dollars, but I think in LeBron's eyes, he sees the need to provide an example to others. I respect that because I know there are many things to do other than let his five-year-old daughter have a YouTube channel. He posted a video on it of them cooking. I think LeBron sees the responsibility of being there for her, and that shows his manhood.

I believe there needs to be more educational programs for young fathers who did not plan to have a child with a young woman but got her pregnant. We need to educate these young men on how to be in the kids' lives and have a relationship with the mother. They need to be taught how to get through personal problems—you cannot hit a target if you cannot see it. How can we expect these young men to grow up to be good fathers when they never saw an example of one?

Some men like my father, who did not have a father, change it around. But he is the exception, not the rule. Reality is that most young men, who grow up without their father present, will grow up not being present in their kids' lives.

The final important quality to understand about the character and integrity of manhood is faith. Growing up we had a reverence of God. I do not say that just because I am Christian. Many young men do not have faith in themselves. They do not believe they can turn a situation around or can be whoever they want to be. That will be huge if we can have these three qualities in our life: show them how to be present, have presence, and have faith.

It is important to introduce these to our kids at a young age. We are what we are exposed to. Let me give you an example. My son plays baseball and is the only black kid on the team. We just moved to this area a couple of years ago. I thought, "Where are all the brothers at?" Then basketball season came along, and guess who was out there? There was only one white kid on his team. So, I analyzed it and thought, "It is not that black people are not good at baseball. We are not out there because we mainly play basketball." A conclusion did not hit me in the sense of sports, but it did when it comes to *exposure.*

We do *not expose* our kids to a variety of activities and experiences. Let's substitute baseball for financial literacy. It's not that we are not smart enough; learning about finances is just *not exposed* to our kids. Faith is *not exposed*. How to be a great father is *not exposed*. You are looking at a generation that underperforms and underachieves, not because of aptitude, but because of lack of exposure. My son is one of the best players on his baseball team. It is not that our young black boys do not want to play baseball. There is a lack of exposure to the sport.

The three important components that should be exposed to our kids are to understand having faith, learning useful options like academics, and having a positive father. I was encouraged to write my first book titled *My Secret Super Power* because of my son. It is about how each child is uniquely gifted. The reason I wrote the book was everyone who saw my son Trey said, "Is he going to be a football or basketball player?" The comments got so annoying that it finally rubbed me the wrong way. People were filling my son's mind with the idea that he should be playing football or basketball. President Theodore Roosevelt said, "People do not care how much you know until they know how much you care." By writing the book, I wanted to show my son and other children that there are more options in life than sports. *Exposure* is key to their success.

T.E.A.M. Manhood Golden Standard: Being *present* is one key to manhood, and having *presence* is significant. *Exposure* is the key to their success. "People do not care how much you know until they know how much you care." Faith is not exposed. How to be a great father is not exposed. You are looking at a generation that underperforms and under-achieves, not because of aptitude, but be-cause of lack of exposure.

GETTING BACK IN THE FIGHT

By Mike Sexton

When I was much younger, I didn't appreciate my father as much as I do today. For years I saw him as a failure and felt that he quit. I had recurring dreams that I was my father's boxing manager telling him to "Get up off the mat!" I repeatedly yelled, "Don't quit now! Don't stop fighting!"

My father fell into a bottle and couldn't find his way out. Why? I don't know, but my guess is we shared a similar struggle. I fell into an ageless lie trap. I was being held captive by the lie that we (men) are to be in control and not ask for help. God forbid if you were to ask for directions.

In my twenties I wandered from job to job in search of significance and acceptance. When I became a jokester, people thought I was funny—but it was still not enough. I felt empty. In my mid-thirties, I moved across the country putting my old life behind me. With a new wife and my new life, I still struggled because I was running instead of addressing the real issue…me.

I had become a hotshot working with one of the larger studios in Los Angeles. Moving to the opposite side of the country I now had no influence, no friends, and no one to confide in. I needed someone to confide in besides my wife. These were men's issues. I needed my dad. I became a big drinker trying to drown my problems. Drinking was an exit that allowed me to not take responsibility for my issues. The alcohol distorted my vision to the point it clouded my judgment. I could no longer see who I looked at in the mirror.

Then one freezing night I lost my jacket, keys, and wallet. God seized the moment to reveal that He gave it all to me, and He could easily take it all away. My jacket disappeared when I put it down somewhere. I don't know why I didn't put it behind the bar like every other night. My coat provided warmth, comfort, and protection from the cold. My keys were my shelter...all of my belongings. My wallet was gone...no money or credit cards. My identification? How could I prove who I was?

I slept off my dilemma at my drinking buddy's room in a nearby produce store. The concrete floor froze from the nineteen degrees overnight low. My friend only had his sleeping bag, so my lost jacket meant I was without a blanket too. Somehow, later that day I was able to pay a locksmith a fraction of what it would have cost in the wee hours of the morning. I got into my house to find a spare key, take a shower, and change clothes. I felt I was being punked, still fuzzy from the case of beer consumed the night before. I felt lost and all alone. There was nowhere to go to get away from myself. I couldn't escape. My life was consumed by frustration, panic, and self-doubt.

That evening, hung over, I went to a men's retreat as promised. There were five men at our church who invited me. They were trying to save me, but I couldn't (or wouldn't) be saved.

My wife gave me a note before she left town for answers to her own questions. She instructed me to not open it until we got to the retreat. I put the note in my suitcase and forgot about it as my compadres and I drove out of the city into the foothills. I was in new territory and didn't recognize the beauty of the Blue Ridge because I didn't know where I was.

My Christian brothers Geoff, Bud, Jim, Tony, and John tried to comfort me on the drive. I was on edge and hypersensitive to what I was experiencing. These guys made themselves available to me. I just didn't know how to ask for help. We all found seats in the back of the hall. To this day I have no idea what Pastor Peter Lord preached about, but without realizing it, I headed to the front of the room.

God knew I had to get to a point of surrender. Turning the keys to my life over to Christ was my best choice. I soon found myself in a secluded garden talking directly to God. He reminded me of the note, and I went to my cabin and read it. My wife shared in the tear-stained letter that she was ready to give up on us unless I made a change. Again, God reminded me that He could take everyone and everything away from me.

What God did that night was take away the old me. He saved me. Not only for Himself, but He saved me from my old self. My father died in 1995, and I wasn't there to say goodbye or tell him that I loved him. My relationship with him was so damaged that my pride wouldn't allow me to call him. My shame in how I treated my dad was too great to overcome.

As I find myself closer to the end of my days here on earth than the beginning of my life, I have come to realize that God placed me here for His purpose. Not mine. That purpose right now is to let you know that God didn't create us to then drop us on our head. He loves us so much that He is willing to put Himself in harm's way to save us.

I didn't realize at the time of my surrender to Him that He is in complete control. I was still trying to control my depression and lack of self-confidence. He knows I needed to give Him everything, including my relationship with my earthly father. My father wasn't always available physically or emotionally. Our Father in heaven is always available and willing to fight for every one of us. What does that mean? It means we do not have to sweat the small stuff. It means that God knew exactly what He was doing when He created us, including our family members. He places us with the people we interact with every single day because He has a purpose for that encounter. The beauty is He trusts you with that interaction. He created you for that very moment. God knows every struggle and achievement we will experience. He knows when it will go to our head, how we will react to any acknowledgement of our actions, or how we will respond to the challenges we face.

One of the greatest challenges in my life was during my late teens and early twenties. I struggled with living at home with my parents. Being one of eleven children, my parents were overwhelmed financially and emotionally. Because of that they had a very hard time letting go. As a man, the greatest struggles have come when I felt most vulnerable. When I feel vulnerable, I feel alone. And when I feel alone, fear tends to overtake me. That fear is due to the lie that we are supposed to be in control and not ask for help.

When asked, "What are three viewpoints that are needed in manhood in today's modern society?" I list them as follows:

1. We are not designed to live alone. Not long ago I met a man named William. He was in his early forties and freshly out of a State Penitentiary where he spent twenty years for murder. When William was seventeen, he shot a young man who abused a female classmate. William thought that shooting this guy was an honorable action because he felt he was protecting his friend. He didn't know that his own life would be forever changed. Today William will tell you that his twenty-year sentence was due to not having anyone to talk to. He was fending for himself on the streets of New York and bought the lie that he was in control of his own life and didn't need any help. That lie cost him twenty precious years.

2. We need to extend grace to one another. My earthly father extends me a tremendous amount of grace putting up with my selfishness. He didn't know how to extend that same grace to himself. He never forgave himself for his own failures, and he didn't know that God's grace was available to him. I didn't know how to extend grace to my dad because I never experienced it from him. It was only from my heavenly Father that I experienced grace when He forgave me of my sins. He wants to do that for you, too.

3. We cannot be afraid to ask for help or admit we are wrong. Do not be afraid to ask for help. Seek out a male friend so you can help each other. Sometimes our fathers are not available. Find a positive male role model to spend time with you. If you do not have a father, ask God to be your Father. He is always available. He wants to love you and help you throughout your life. Do not be afraid to admit when you are wrong. We all fail from time to time. Did you know that Jesus fell three times carrying the cross to His death? Where would we be if Jesus quit? We would all be lost.

My dad was a special person. He was an encouragement, yet he wasn't always available because of the battles and challenges in his own life. I didn't realize that until I surrendered my life to Christ. Now I know that we are here to help each other and pick each other up to get back in the fight.

T.E.A.M. Manhood Golden Standard: Never be afraid to ask for help or admit you are wrong. Extending grace to one another as men is important for connection. We are not designed to be alone. Building a bond with other men is key to your significant growth. If you fall, always gain the strength to get back up! My dad was a special person. He was an encouragement, yet he wasn't always available because of the battles and challenges in his own life. I didn't realize that until I surrendered my life to Christ. Now I know that we are here to help each other and pick each other up to get back in the fight.

INTEGRITY IN THE NEW MILLENNIUM

By Kendall Taylor

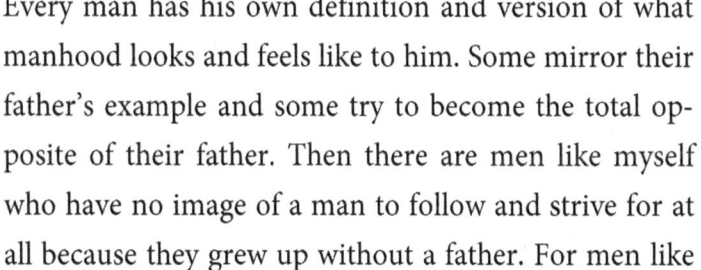

Every man has his own definition and version of what manhood looks and feels like to him. Some mirror their father's example and some try to become the total opposite of their father. Then there are men like myself who have no image of a man to follow and strive for at all because they grew up without a father. For men like me, we often reach to become a version of manhood that we have never seen with our own eyes.

I have never been greedy for power or money. I believe that is the reason God has allowed me the grace to obtain and manage both with integrity. I wanted to be a man that other men admired and respected. It was less about having a gravitational pull with women than having the strength and wisdom to lead men. To me there is no greater task on earth that a man can try to master than to lead other men.

In order to be able to lead men, I first must be able to govern my family and myself. There was a time where I lost all that I had including my family, money, and power. I didn't complain and blame others for my condition. I took inventory of my mistakes and the decisions that led me into a season of disaster and began to design and rebuild my life once again.

Over the course of a seven-year period, I was able to restore all my key relationships, change my posture and perspectives as a man, shift my reputation in the community and marketplace, and acquire ownership in several businesses. My personal recognition of when I knew I was a man was in carrying out what very few men have been able to do. I lost everything and rebuilt something even greater without compromising my name and integrity. I proved to God and myself that I could survive on this earth as a leader. As long as I trusted God, all of my gifts and talents would continue to make room for me and bring me in large rooms in the company of great men. This for me was my sign of officially entering the portal to manhood!

Men today as a whole, but not all, have separated themselves from the spirit of integrity. As a nation of men, we have compromised our integrity in attempts to obtain fame, wealth, or fulfill our lustful desires due to an inability to display self-control over matters of temptation and the flesh. The massive MeToo movement is a testament to that fact. This wave of accountability from abused women was not as much eye opening as it was simply the hidden truth that remained beneath the surface finally being exposed and accountability being enforced.

There is a male condition that I label **EMS.** I believe it captures the three main issues that obstruct men from walking in the fullness of integrity.

Emotions: Men are not effectively trained in emotional management while women are trained from birth. If women cannot manage them, they can at least find them and be aware of their existence. If a little girl sits in the corner crying, either parent will rush to her side, comfort her, and stop at no end to get to the bottom of the source behind her tears. If a little boy cries, he is trained to "suck it up" and very little attention is given to peeling back the layers of his emotions to help him navigate through the feelings that overwhelm him.

Therefore, we ignore our emotions by suppressing them. Anything that a man simply ignores will in time turn and rule him and all his decisions. Poor emotional management prevents men from walking in integrity because integrity hinges on a man's ability to emotionally decipher between right and wrong in a world that does not tend to celebrate the latter.

Money: Money alone is not the root of all evil. The spirit of greed is the root that takes hold of the concept of money and in time grows branches to become a tree of evilness! The greatest mechanism of compromise among men today is money. Money presents itself as the ideal source of power, which all men secretly desire. But when power is not assigned a positive and sacrificial mission, it will naturally bend toward a spirit of manipulation and lordship over others. Men are too willing to cut corners and throats to get a leap over another man because they are unwilling to endure the due process of natural evolution to success. Integrity is lost when men entertain illegal means and unjust tactics for their own personal agendas and timeline as they attempt to expedite God's plan. Integrity will not take a bribe that will bring pollution to a system. Integrity will refuse to tear down the reputation of another in order to build one's own name.

But this is not what we see happening today. From the stock exchange, big banks, small business, and even local and mega churches, we continue to see scandals come to light bringing shock and disappointment. Sadly, these are only the examples that have been exposed while other schemes are still alive and uncovered. Money alone does not rob a man of integrity and character; it simply supplies a means for unethical men to showcase their character flaws in style and glamour.

Sex: My, how many nations, civilizations, countries, and even governments have been compromised because of the sexual immorality of men! Even in attempts to search through the Bible, it is almost impossible to find men who could stand with integrity when faced with the threat of sexual temptation. There is one that comes to mind who stood firm and endured great affliction for holding on to his integrity…his name was Joseph.

He was sold off into slavery from his brothers and wrongfully imprisoned having committed no crime. Joseph remained committed to God throughout his ordeal, and it was his integrity that lifted him from the depths of prison and placed him at the feet of service to Potiphar (a very wealthy and powerful dignitary in Egypt). Once again, his integrity remained strong when he was bestowed power and authority. While in possession of these gifts, he expressed even greater demonstrations of integrity by carrying out his tasks and the management of great affairs with wisdom and self-restraint.

Pharaoh's wife threw herself at Joseph, and he continued to brush off her sexual advances. At this scene in Joseph's story, I need to pause and make a very powerful and underestimated point. In a world full of men who live beneath the threshold of integrity, those who make the sacrifices to uphold the line will be attractive and desirable to women who will see you as a precious jewel among men. This could have been the very moment that Joseph chose to entertain compromise and cross the line of integrity. Instead, this young giant refrained from laying a finger on Potiphar's wife, even when she lied claiming that he tried to rape her and Joseph was once again thrown into prison.

No matter how delicious a meal is that's placed before a man of integrity, he alone has control to make the decision of whether to fill his belly with what is being served or push his plate and rise from the table. Too often men make excuses for the actions of others before taking full responsibility for the actions they conduct themselves.

Three Qualities that are needed in Manhood in Today's Modern Society

1. ACCOUNTABILITY: Men young and old are dropping the ball by not making a contribution to the nation of men. Young men are not trustworthy, don't honor their word, and don't complete most of anything that they start. Our young men are emotionally weak and bail on anything that confronts them as a challenge. They don't chase education and wisdom but turn to the streets thinking it is a sign of strength when it is truly the opposite. They need to be accountable to the communities and people they impact as leeches, instead of producers and providers.

Elders drop the ball by withholding wisdoms and secret passageways, refusing to pass the torch to the younger generation. It's fair that young men have to be proven ill prepared to receive such precious gifts. But when suitable candidates are found, there is hesitancy and reluctance to move out of the chair and allow young and innovative minds the opportunity to lead the next generation. Elders must be accountable to pass the torch and make it a mission to seek candidates out if they are not within reach. This cycle between both generations is broken and needs to be repaired before we wake up destroyed and lost as a race of weak men!

2. A MISSION: Men need a purpose that is filled with great challenge and great reward. There are droves of men that can be found hanging around bars, street corners, strip clubs, and other places that bear no fruit or productivity. Men need to war and battle for something that is greater than themselves because it is in this place—and this place alone—that they are forced to tap into their abilities that would not be provoked otherwise. Men are awakened when they reach the end of themselves and are forced to activate an unknown energy source that we all possess deep inside. It seems so boring and cliché, but it stays true that where there is no pain, there is no gain!

All great men that we admire and respect today attached themselves to a cause or a mission that required their undivided and relentless attention where they removed all distractions and dedicated themselves to a single purpose. When a man believes in something and commits in his heart to see it through, the hours of study, practice, networking, training, and preparation seem miniscule in the grand scope of the goal in mind.

3. ROUNDTABLE: Men need other men! At times we pursue tasks and try to climb mountains that seem impossible to overcome. Having strong like-minded men who can encourage, uplift, support, and challenge us along the way is instrumental. I would not be where I am sitting today without key male relationships that I respected enough to allow them to constructively criticize me, hold me accountable, and encourage me in some very challenging times in my life. Men must wash away the idea that they can reach levels of success in manhood alone. And not just manhood but also in fatherhood, marriage, business, faith, and any step along the journey. Each step presents its own obstacles to overcome to walk as a man.

Men need men that they can trust, lean on, and even have weak moments in confidence and trust. Every President has his Vice, every General his Captains, and even Christ had His Disciples. All men need other men to carry out living as a man of integrity!

T.E.A.M. Manhood Golden Standard: Every man with character and integrity needs to be accountable and have an accountability partner. Men must find their mission in life that will lead to their purpose. A key ingredient for a man of the 21st century is to be part of a roundtable or group of men to share in confidence, achieve wisdom, and be encouraged. Men need men that they can trust, lean on, and even have weak moments in confidence and trust. Every President has his Vice, every General his Captains, and even Christ had His Disciples. All men need other men to carry out living as a man of integrity! Men are awakened when they reach the end of themselves and are forced to activate an unknown energy source that we all possess deep inside. It seems so boring and cliché, but it stays true that where there is no pain, there is no gain!

GENERATIONAL MAN

By Chris Graham

I understand why men might feel frustrated. It's a hard piece of news to find out we can't simply shift our personal behavior and call sexism and racism fixed. It's a dark realization to find out that despite all our efforts, we have still only scratched the surface of truly understanding the trauma being inflicted globally on women, men of color, immigrants, and children.

We are a generation of men tasked with addressing ongoing, systemic trauma—both ours and others. We are burdened with accepting the brutal realizations of #MeToo, #BlackLivesMatter, and the ugly outbreak of white nationalism across Europe and America. Waves of catastrophic trauma are the result of generational box culture. Because of how man box culture has bullied and conditioned men, we have been stripped of the capacities we need to repair the damage done. We have suppressed in boys and men our deeply human capacities for empathy, emotional expression, collaboration, and connection. In the beautiful human conversation, we have been bullied and brutalized into disconnection and isolation. All in the pursuit of proving we are "real men." We have been cheated out of human connection by a culture of manhood that tells us independence is the most vaunted of masculine traits, that hiding our emotions makes us strong, and that being dominant is the only course of action that will keep us safe.

But dominance won't keep us safe. The wounded world around us is the result of thousands of years of relying on models of dominance. Healing damage on the scale of what we are confronting will not happen through emotional stoicism, toughness, independence, sexual prowess, or any of the other acclaimed assets of generational man box culture. But the vast majority of men know of no other tools to apply to our shaking, shuddering world, and so we are becoming increasingly reactive and alarmed.

Generational man box culture teaches us to never show self-doubt, never admit we are wrong, and always have the last word. It teaches us to align ourselves with hierarchical pecking orders of dominance as a way to construct our social institutions. It teaches us to rely on power created *over* others instead of power created *with* others. But it's a model for human society that doesn't work.

And so, men's anger surges up in the disconnect between the privileges that we continue to exercise every day and the calamity that is modern life. Surely this is someone else's fault. Immigrants. Socialists. Feminists. No. It is not. This is entirely on our dominant culture of masculinity, formed and framed by the generational man box. This is on us. As hard as it may be to own that, we must own it if we are to save our children and grandchildren from despair and hopelessness.

Generational manhood is not so much about anatomy and age as it is about a particular type of character. If we did not all have a general idea that manhood is a definite and distinct identity, the statement "He is not a man" would have little meaning. But it has immediate meaning, and we take those words as a strong rebuke upon the person. Manhood is distinct, and this is necessary to understand when you consider what makes a man.

What are the character qualities that mark healthy manhood? To be genuine, the qualities that mark manhood should apply generally to men across diverse cultures, not just our own. This reveals what God has placed in all humanity and what He has made the man to be, not just what any particular culture expects. As we seek to bring young men into healthy and authentic manhood, we must ask, "What are we shooting for, and what does doing this look like when done successfully?"

This question can be more complex than many assume. One can be a "good man" and quite different in temperament, talents, and interests than other men. Martin Luther King Jr. was a different kind of "good man" than evangelist Dr. Myles Munroe. Retired General Colin Powell is not President Obama. But these differences do not mean we cannot speak meaningfully and truthfully about what manhood is and is not. Good men do have basic common qualities.

While certainly not exhaustive or comprehensive, this list is a compilation of many of the most important, widely practiced, and culturally expected qualities of manhood. Cultural anthropologists, psychologists, and sociologists who have studied the nature of manhood across diverse cultures and time recognize these traits.

Courage: A man does not shrink from a necessary challenge, regardless of risk. He will face danger, difficulty, and self-denial when called upon for the sake of others.

Step Up: A man is the first one out of his seat (figuratively and literally) when a need arises. He's a problem solver and takes initiative. Passivity is never manly.

Provide and Protect: A man has learned how, and is willing to provide and care for, a particular woman and their common children. He doesn't skip out on this duty. Even if he never marries, he's the kind of person who could do this and provides for others in various ways. As anthropologist David Gilmore concludes, "A man produces more than he consumes," and the community benefits from his work and generosity.

Self-Reliance: A man can stand on his own and not need to depend on others for his well-being. The greatness of a man is not in how much wealth he acquires, but in his integrity and ability to positively affect those around him. Moral authority comes from following universal and timeless principles like honesty, integrity, and treating people with respect. He is not a loner though. He is willing to work with others.

Honesty and Moral Strength: A man does what is right and calls out others who do not. He deals with others in integrity. Temptation presents itself to every man, but the decisions and actions he takes in light of it significantly determine his manhood. He can be trusted to do what is right when no one is watching. He keeps his word and is dependable to others.

Tenacity: A man does not easily give up or shrink away in the face of challenge or adversity. He sticks with it and wants to overcome obstacles. "It can't be done" doesn't come to him easily.

Self-Control: A man is aware of the proper limits for himself—his strength, appetites, independence, language, and power—and respects them. He calls others to do the same.

Under Authority: A man recognizes he is under the authority of another—be it a boss, his own father, his pastor, and God—and acts accordingly. He is willing to respectfully challenge those in authority when conscience demands, but he is never simply a renegade.

Shows Respect: A good man shows respect to himself and those he meets, regardless of their situation. He looks them in the eye. Gives another man a firm handshake. Offers words of respect such as "Yes sir/ma'am" or "Thank you, sir." A man helps others feel valuable.

Loyalty: A man is loyal to his family, friends, and others who are close to him, even at great price to himself.

Humility: A man esteems others as valuable and lifts them up. He does not praise himself. He understands the importance of and strength in apologizing and asking forgiveness when he has offended or let others down.

Compassion: This might seem a feminine quality, but a man sees the struggles of the weak and those in trouble and readily comes to their aid. This is a moral strength. A man doesn't exploit an innocent person's weakness.

He Lives His Character: Lastly, if manhood is a distinct set of character traits, the final quality is that he lives them out in action, and he does so conspicuously in the community.A true man will learn from his past generations of men and improve from adolescence to manhood. He will grow and become a man with the utmost character and integrity.

T.E.A.M. Manhood Golden Standard: A man is aware of the proper limits for himself—his strength, appetites, independence, language, and power—and respects them. He calls others to do the same. A man esteems other as valuable and lifts them up. He does not praise himself. He understands the importance of and strength in apologizing and asking forgiveness when he has offended or let others down. A man does not shrink from a necessary challenge, regardless of risk. He will face danger, difficulty, and self-denial when called upon for the sake of others. Manhood is a distinct set of character traits, and the final quality is that he lives them out in action, and he does so conspicuously in the community.

A true man will learn from his past generations of men and improve from adolescence to manhood. He will grow and become a man with the utmost character and integrity.

SUCCESS DRIVEN

By Jervay Vanderhorst

Men of integrity are learners. They lead the pack by learning the strengths of the pack. Being a man of integrity teaches you to treat individuals with respect no matter who they are. There is no way to walk with a light shining within you if you are not willing to shine that light on others.

My integrity was challenged and displayed when I got booked to work an event in Las Vegas as a Production Assistant. I was the lowest of the low on the staff depth chart, but I carried myself like I mattered...I was taught to act like you belong. Even when I was given a job that most workers would not want to do, I did the task like it was the most important assignment ever. I was treated with respect in return.

Primary sclerosing cholangitis (PSC) is a chronic, or long-term, disease that slowly damages the bile ducts. Approximately one in ten thousand people have it. PSC made me realize my manhood quickly. I was diagnosed between the ages of thirteen to fourteen years old and was forced to look at life differently at a young age. It has now shaped how I act in my adult life.

The liver condition taught me to appreciate life, cherish it, live and not just exist. At thirteen, I had to learn the real meaning of prayer and faith. I learned the importance of survival and optimism. PSC shaped me to value healthy eating and helped me develop healthy eating habits. I also started to monitor what I put in my body; this allowed me not to depend on medicine. Food became my medicine.

I define manhood with 4 P's: ***Prioritizing* your *Potential* to find your *Passion* and *Purpose***. It's that simple to me. Once you figure out those important factors, you will mature into the man you need to become. Make your goals your *priority*. Whatever you have the *potential* to do should be accomplished. The way to maximize potential is to work on each priority daily. We prioritize everything else…our spouse, kids, bills, hobbies, etc. But are you making your talent, the God given gift that you have, your priority and are you pursuing it?

Your *passion* comes from what you love. What you do with no effort. Things that make you smile have no price tag and can you bring an abundance of joy.

Your *purpose* is defined by asking yourself, "What is my life mission? What am I here to accomplish before I leave this earth?" Ask yourself this... Think about it... We all have a purpose. WHAT'S YOURS? And what are you doing daily to find out what that is?

Today's society needs love. Men are not necessarily taught how to love or how to receive it. Every situation is different. There are some men that are taught love because they are surrounded by it. They learn it because they see it or have been shown love in their life. It's hard to learn how to love if you haven't experienced it already yourself. Many parents show their sons love, and some parents don't. Once the love is shown, it's totally up to the individual to recognize it, receive it, and reciprocate it. In its absence the world reflects the need for love.

We also need true leaders, not attention seekers. Some of us are being influenced into a land of toxic waste just because everyone is following certain trends.

Love is something I know all about. I've been shown love my entire life, so I give it back to the universe. From my family, friends, or people that I've shown love to, they can feel that it's genuine because I give it effortlessly. It's all I know.

Leadership is not about power. It means being responsible, caring, understanding, generous, and one of integrity. No one will want to follow a leader that does not hold themselves accountable first. Lead by example. More action and fewer words. Be a man. Live it. Walk it. Become it. True leaders may not get the recognition, awards, or the accolades but their spirit wins something much greater. You get love in return for leading. To me love is the most powerful emotion that you can share or receive.

I'm influenced by love…the entire planet is. Everyone loves someone or something. Plants can't grow if the soil is not tended to, and that's how our hearts are. It's love in us all; we just have to choose wisely whom we share that love with!

T.E.A.M. Manhood Golden Standard: I define manhood with 4 P's: Prioritizing your Potential to find your Passion and Purpose. It's that simple to me. Once you figure out those important factors, you will mature into the man you need to become. Leadership is not about power. It means being responsible, caring, understanding, generous, and one of integrity. No one will want to follow a leader that does not hold themselves accountable first. Lead by example. More action and fewer words. Be a man. Live it. Walk it. Become it. True leaders may not get the recognition, awards, or the accolades but their spirit wins something much greater. You get love in return for leading.

CHARACTER AND THE INTEGRITY OF A MAN

By Peter Adamson

A man is made of God after His likeness which means man is to function like God, look from the eye of God, have an understanding of God, and must be completely obedient to God. The first man created was given a certain instruction on how to live, what to eat, etc. He abides by the commandment of God. He thinks like God, and that is why he was able to name all the animals in the Garden according to God's instruction. The name Adam gave to all animals is what they are called today.

Now, let us look at this word found in the Bible that described the characters of man. Proverbs 24:27 says, "Prepare your outside work, Make it fit for yourself in the field; And afterward build your house."

From the Scripture above, you are not allowed to build your house—I mean marry—without first of all building yourself. Which means you need to graduate from school, find a job, and take care of things that matter in life; then you can now build your house.

Preparation is required in every facet of life; and without it, failure is bound to take place. Jesus mentions this in the New Testament in John 5:17. "My Father works, and hitherto work I." I must do the work of Him that sent me.

God loves preparations. God gives little but to preparations. All His own great works He has done preparedly. Creation was not done without great forethought (Proverbs 8:27-31). And redemption was no sudden after-thought—before the foundation of the earth was laid, redemption was cast in the mind of God. Every event that happens to every man was planned ages before the man was born. The children of Israel did not enter Canaan until they had gone through a preparatory discipline. Neither did prophets, nor apostles, nor Jesus Himself begin work without an interval of solitude and discipline for perfect readiness. The preparation of Jesus was marvelous.

Within the compass of this present world, everything is placed in the state and order that it is to fit us for something that is coming afterwards. Just as in a good education every rule leads up to a higher rule, and every new piece of knowledge is the basis of another piece so that the mind is always being made ready for something beyond it, so it is in God's dispensations. A joy may be a prelude to a sorrow, or a sorrow may be a prelude to a joy, or a joy to a higher joy, or a sorrow to a still deeper sorrow. Nothing is isolated. It is not isolated joy; it is not isolated sorrow. The great responsibility we have is to be careful that we treat everything as preparatively. We should always be asking, when joy and sorrow comes, "Of what is the precursor? What is God going to do with me next?"

Let the preparation suit what you are going to do—a general preparation for general duty—but a special preparation for things special. The materials you gather in the "field" must be suited to the particular "house" which you are going to "build." Always make a stop upon the eve, and search into your own heart and say, "Am I ready? Has God given me a true preparation?" If not, as far as you can, stop a little longer before you take another step. Whatever you do, secure preparation before you begin. There is a frame of mind that is in a continual preparedness. It is the "Here I am!" of the patriarchs. It is a high, blessed state. (*J. Vaughan, M.A.*)

Another vital point that makes a man is diligence. Proverbs 22:29 says, "Seest thou a man diligent in his business? He shall stand before kings and not mean men." The first man was committed to the module of his destiny and also to the work of his community. God does not commit another assignment to any man who refuses to fulfill the first assignment. In Genesis you will discover that after Adam fulfilled the first assignment, God fulfilled his need, and then He committed another assignment to him.

My first sentence said that to be a man of integrity, you must be completely obedient to God. In Joshua 1:2 after the death of Moses, the LORD said to Moses' aide Joshua, "Moses my servant is dead. Now then, you and all these people, get ready to cross the Jordan River into the land I am about to give to them—to the Israelites." When you look into the story, you will discover that Joshua was not ready, and he trusted God. In Joshua 1:8 God gave him instructions, "This Book of the Law shall not depart from your mouth, but you shall meditate on it day and night, so that you may be careful to do according to all that is written in it. For then you will make your way prosperous, and then you will have good success." When you read further, you discover that Joshua follows what God told him. To be a man of integrity, you must be obedient.

When I was growing up, I learned that what makes a man is not fathering a baby, marrying a wife, or even being wealthy. What makes a real man is the ability to lead others, lead communities, and develop society.

When I was married anew, after a year my wife joined me here in America. A certain woman from our church called me and said, "I think you are a man not knowing that you are far away from one. If you are a man, you could have got your wife pregnant by now." At that time, I was already a pastor with a lot of people under my umbrella as a shepherd. I had more than five children in the university, paid their tuition, and made sure that they have a good life…even though I chose them on the street and decided to help them. I also had a program in my local area to feed the hungry. To be a good man, you must be ready to serve others.

T.E.A.M. Manhood: Encouragement

Proverbs 42:1-2 says, "As the deer panteth after the water brooks, so panteth my soul after thee, O God. My soul thirsteth for God, for the living God. When shall I come and appear before God?" Every man should desire to know of God, to do His will, and to obey His commandment for that is the will of God for us.

Deuteronomy 28:1-14 tells us that we can enjoy the goodness of the Lord.

"If you fully obey the LORD your God and carefully follow all His commands I give you today, the LORD your God will set you high above all the nations on earth. ² All these blessings will come on you and accompany you if you obey the LORD your God. ³ You will be blessed in the city and blessed in the country. ⁴ The fruit of your womb will be blessed, and the crops of your land and the young of your livestock—the calves of your herds and the lambs of your flocks. ⁵ Your basket and your kneading trough will be blessed. ⁶ You will be blessed when you come in and blessed when you go out. ⁷ The LORD will grant that the enemies who rise up against you will be defeated before you. They will come at you from one direction but flee from you in seven. ⁸ The LORD will send a blessing on your barns and on everything you put your hand to. The LORD your God will bless you in the land he is giving you. ⁹ The LORD will establish you as His holy people, as He promised you on oath, if you keep the commands of the LORD your God and walk in obedience to Him. ¹⁰ Then all the peoples on earth will see that you are called by the name of the LORD, and they will fear you. ¹¹ The LORD will grant you abundant prosperity—in the fruit of your womb, the young of your livestock and the crops of your ground—in the land He swore to your ancestors to give you. ¹² The LORD will open the heavens, the storehouse of His bounty, to send rain on your land in season and to bless all the work of your hands. You will lend to many nations but will borrow from none. ¹³ The LORD will make you the head, not the tail. If you pay attention to the commands of the LORD your God that I give you this day and carefully follow them, you will always be at the top, never at the bottom. ¹⁴ Do not turn aside from any of the commands I give you today, to the right or to the left, following other gods and serving them. Shalom"

T.E.A.M. Manhood Golden Standard: A vital point that makes a man is diligence. Proverbs 22:29 says, "Seest thou a man diligent in his business. He shall stand before kings and not mean men." The first man was committed to the module of his destiny and to the work of his community. God does not commit another assignment to any man who refuses to fulfill the first assignment.

LEVERAGE

By Harold Sendar

---ɔ◠ɔ---

When will I create a solid foundation in my career?
When will I be financially free from hardship?
When will I meet my soulmate and get married?
When will I have kids?

What is my purpose and when will I start operating within my gift?

These are the thoughts that seem to cluster our young adult minds as we desperately try to find the answers through trial and error. There is a false reality that we will all have life figured out by a certain age. It is almost as though there is this perception that you need to have a four-year degree, get married, have kids, as well as become a homeowner…all before age thirty. The issue here is that as individuals we need to leverage our own thoughts, feelings, and experiences instead of being driven by social trends and approval. Oftentimes we find ourselves comparing our lives to that of others based on *their* opinions or beliefs.

In order to fulfill God's purpose in your life, you must not be controlled by others opinions. Recognize that the path and destiny that God has given you is not only your unique pathway to success, but it is also where motherhood or manhood is birthed. Henry David Thoreau said, "The value of any experience is measured, of course, not by the amount of money, but the amount of development we get out of it. I think that no experience which I have today comes up to, or is comparable with, the experiences of my boyhood." The takeaway message here is that the lessons we learn from our experiences, and the character that is developed as a byproduct, is what defines manhood.

According to the NAACP, "Statistics show that more than thirty percent of African Americans represent those in the legal system." As a son of two parents with postgraduate degrees, as well as a father with a military background, I struggled with facing the fact that I put myself in a position where I became a part of the statistics.

I will never forget that day. "You will never be successful, and you can forget about school," said Officer Meadows. I thought to myself, "How could I make such a mistake?" My parents did absolutely nothing wrong to me in order to deserve that level of embarrassment from their child. My mother was characterized as caring, strong minded, and independent. She had an educational background in healthcare administration and social work. My father was more reserved, hard working, and ambitious. He was retired military with an educational background in both public health and nursing.

My mind was clouded with the thought that I would never amount to anything successful due to past mistakes. I struggled with depression and ultimately had feelings of inadequacy. Despite all this negative thinking and emotions, I managed to attend East Carolina University and graduated with a Bachelor's Degree in Public Health. Although on the outside I seemed stoic in nature and always positive, at my core I was hesitant and fearful walking into my next chapter of life. As an undergraduate student, everyone understands that post graduating the first objective is to get a job. As for me I knew my experience would be different. I understood by the odds being against me that my employment would be contingent upon whatever my employer's perception of me was on paper.

Finally the day came that I had anticipated for so long. I had my first interview, and I was ecstatic to even have the opportunity—a lot of my colleagues were employed doing something unrelated to their degree or field of study. I vividly remember the director saying, "Harold, you interviewed very well, and I am sure you will get the job."

A couple weeks later I received a letter in the mail. It read, "Dear Mr. Sendar. Thank you for your interest in the Head Start Program Coordinator position. There were many qualified candidates who applied, and we have decided to choose someone else. Best of luck on your job search." I was completely distraught. Within weeks I had another employment opportunity only to have the same cut opened again. I could not help but to think to myself, "Is this going to keep happening? Who is going to give me a chance?"

At this point in my life, my mind seemed to be in survival mode. I wanted to save as much money as I could as a defense mechanism. Truth be told, every time I looked in the mirror I saw a reflection of the insecurities within myself. Until one day I made the decision to change the direction of my life. I had to fix the issues at my core, and that meant changing the direction of my thinking.

I watched a motivational video by Pastor Eric Thomas called "Push Past the Pain." I compare the message Thomas delivered to motherhood and childbirth. The same way a mother has to endure past pain to deliver her child is the same way an individual has to push past his or her trials and tribulations to see the fruits of their labor. It all made sense to me at this moment. I needed to refocus my energy on what was most important. The two most important adjustments I needed to make were to foster positive and healthy relationships in my life and leverage my faith.

During my time at East Carolina University I became heavily involved in the community and created numerous networking opportunities and relationships. In addition, I was one of six co-founders who pioneered a nonprofit and campus organization called The T.E.A.M. It stands for **T**alented **E**mpowered **A**spired **M**en. Because of my past, I decided to immerse myself in the T.E.A.M.'s vision in order to recreate the perception of how minority males are seen and reflected in modern society today. I wanted to be a part of the process in which minority males committed to taking their education seriously, as well as transitioning into more prominent roles in their communities.

I foresaw the need to both be a part of and foster healthy relationships not only to heal my core issues but as leverage for my future. Leverage is the means by which an individual has the power to influence a person or situation to achieve a particular outcome. By improving the quality of the relationships around us, we have the advantage of having that same quality to pour into other avenues within our lives. This can include our relationship with God, family, money, friends, and more.

As time went on, I was given the opportunity to work as a mental health counselor. It was ironic to me that a company would employ someone who had been *through* the system to work with individuals with mental and behavioral health needs *in* the system. Never in a million years did I think that the experiences that I went through would be the mouthpiece and the grounds to relate to so many of my clients. For so long I was tainted by the belief that once you went through the system…you are useless. The truth is…your past does not determine your future—your faith does.

Leveraging faith in order to weather the storms in life is an important attribute that we should all possess or tap into. No matter if you believe in a higher power or not, we have all been in a position where there is uncertainty or no guarantee of a particular outcome. In these moments we rely on our faith or hope that things go in our favor. From personal experience—leveraging faith has been my only option.

Once I shifted the direction of my thinking, I began to understand that certain decisions and experiences do not destroy us as individuals. Instead, they actually mold us into the individuals we become. This is the paradigm shift—all our experiences have a reason. Although it is a common cliché, think of how the experiences that you went through in the past benefitted you later.

For example, if it were not for my experience with the legal system, under what circumstances or grounds would I have been able to relate to the specific population I work with today? Would I have been as useful? If it were not for the positive relationships built and established in my undergraduate career, would there have been an impact to leverage? In hindsight, the commonality in the answer to all the previous questions is "No" because every experience played a part in the outcome. Fostering healthy relationships and leveraging faith gave me the energy to propel forward through life's trials and tribulations.

No matter what direction you take in life, it is my belief that your personal experiences prepare and suit you for your destiny. My advice to men today is…leverage.

- Leverage who you are.
- Leverage what you know.
- Leverage every experience in order to get where you need to go.

This is The T.E.AM.: Character and the integrity of manhood.

T.E.A.M. Manhood Golden Standard: In order to fulfill God's purpose in your life, you must not be controlled by the opinions of others. Recognize that the path and destiny that God has given you is not only your unique pathway to success, but it is also where motherhood or manhood is birthed. No matter what direction you take in life, it is my belief that your personal experiences prepare and suit you for your destiny. My advice to men today is…leverage.

- Leverage who you are.
- Leverage what you know.
- Leverage every experience in order to get where you need to go.

This is The T.E.AM.: Character and the integrity of manhood.

GROWN MAN

By Dr. Lathan Turner

Growing up in a small community in the South set the background for my development as a young person in this country. There was an array of examples of manhood that, when I think back, contributed to all youth in town. This scenario I share is relevant to many young men everywhere. It adds context to my experiences of how character and integrity were shaped.

As a youth, my small town consisted of social norms typical of the South in the '60s and '70s. I attended a segregated school system until 7th grade, experienced separatism in certain stores and offices based on race, and went about daily activities trying to understand why this was happening. It did not take long to realize the unusual circumstances because integration happened, and my world changed. It was an abrupt change, but the one thing that provided a source of strength was the "community" instilled in me as a youth.

It was much later that I fully understood what the term *role models* meant. In my "community" were men who worked hard every day to provide for their families. They worked five, six, or seven days a week, generally on average for eight hours, and then came home to check on their families...but their work was not finished. The men were also involved in the church, community, organizations and associations, tended to home or car repairs, coached their kids' teams, and did odd jobs around town. I saw this and admired what they were doing. It was a norm that I expected to see day after day. I saw mentorship in action, but it was more like responsibility in action.

Because I grew up in a community where everyone usually knew each other, I don't remember a specific situation where I "became a man." The process is fluid, and it happens for most young men over the course of time. It may have happened as a result of playing sports, or during a relationship with the opposite sex, or as the result of a difficult family situation.

The transition to high school after integration was easier for me than middle school. From an early age, I knew all my black classmates very well and felt like there was a unique bond with them. I cannot say the same about middle school because there was the unknown and an initial level of distrust with the people who were our new classmates. Only time would help resolve some of that, and we only had four years of school left. So, life would get better, but this was still not what defined my growth into manhood. I can say that there were things that captured my curiosity but not to the level of transitioning to manhood.

I enjoyed most of the experiences from high school such as sports, clubs and organizations, and social interaction. I worked hard to be a part of a lot of activities, almost to my detriment, as I did not live up to my true academic potential. Regardless, I did well, applied for college, and was extremely happy for a chance to move on. Not even working with my father in a cotton mill over the summer was enough for me to claim "manhood" status, although I labored hard enough to realize that I was ready for a new phase of life.

An overview of articles and books written about the *transition to manhood* reveal that the answer to this question of the meaning of manhood remains difficult to translate. In many cases, it is only when the question is intentionally and specifically posed to a male that he begins the psychological process of giving meaning to the question. One researcher, after studying a set of males about becoming a man, stated "The in-depth interviews show the contradictions and uncertainty [these] males have experienced with regard to 'becoming a man.'" [2]

After graduating from high school, it was time for college. I had very high expectations of the college experience. I was not a first-generation college student, but I did not have a full grasp of what was to come. I visited the campus as a youth when my sibling attended, but I was not focused enough to grasp what the future might hold. My parents would later talk with me about the value of going to college, studying hard, and getting a good job. Surely they recognized that I was at the beginning of manhood at another level. It was not my most immediate focus when I went away. At that time, I was more focused on the experience of college than the realization of becoming a man.

Looking back, I can share that my life as a freshman in college was, in fact, the beginning of my transition into becoming a man...a grown man. First, I lived away

---

[2] Crawford, David. *Becoming a Man - The Views and Experiences of Some Second Generation Australian Males.* (University of Western Sydney, Australia, 2003)

from home for more than a couple of days, and that was intriguing. There were new friends, new social outlets, a sprinkle of disappointments, and new academic, as well as personal challenges and opportunities. Each year was a personal development opportunity that I tried my best to manage on a daily basis.

The influence of my "community" when I was growing up, and some of my early experiences there, were part of what defined me as a young man. The difference when I went to college was that I relied on myself more than ever before. I HAD to grow up quickly, make critical decisions, and learn to manage my life. As a freshman, I did not have all the answers. Over the next four years, I found many of them.

Now, almost forty years later, there are many experiences that have become a part of who I am in this society. I have not led the perfect life, but who on earth has? We live and events happen that shape our lives. What becomes important is to find a way, or ways, to take those experiences and share and uplift the next generation of young men who will live and influence others.

I define manhood as a collective of lifetime experiences for males from birth to present existence and how they use them to exist in society. We all go through a series of events that help to inform us of right from wrong, of good from bad, how to move forward, who we depend on, and what we hope to become.

Men should:

Embrace their elders—a lot can be learned and gained from solid relationships with the generation of men who came before us. Conversations with uncles, fathers, grandfathers, godfathers, and community sources are invaluable. The real test of how important they are is when one or more of the resources are no longer around, and a male needs someone to lean on. Some of my fondest moments as a youth were watching and listening to some of those men interact, talk, profess, and function in various spaces. I wish I had an opportunity to tell them what I appreciated at the moment of impact.

Be bridge builders—it is important for males to not be selfish with what they know or have learned. They need to be willing to reach back and help someone else. I have found it to be true that you may never know how much impact you may have on someone else if you are not willing to help others. Exhibit positive traits that influence people. Do not expect numerous accolades for helping others. There is a greater reward for your work if it is genuine, and you will know when the time comes for the proper harvest.

Remain educated—Martin Luther King reminds us that, "The function of education is to teach one to think intensively and to think critically. Intelligence plus character—that is the goal of true education." Men should take the time to read books, research myths AND facts for the truth, discuss with others what has been learned, and put their thoughts in writing to help the next generation.

Life throws many curves at men as they travel the pathways toward manhood. Men should not contribute to their demise but should persevere through all circumstances and remain committed to not just being better, but be the best GROWN man they can be.

T.E.A.M. Manhood Golden Standard:

Men should:

Embrace their elders—a lot can be learned and gained from solid relationships with the generation of men who came before us. Conversations with uncles, fathers, grand-fathers, godfathers, and community sources are invaluable. The real test of how important they are is when one or more of the resources are no longer around, and a male need someone to lean on. Some of my fondest moments as a youth were watching and listening to some of those men interact, talk, profess, and function in various spaces. I wish I had an opportunity to tell them what I appreciated at the moment of impact.

Be bridge builders—it is important for males to not be selfish with what they know or what they have learned. They need to be willing to reach back and help someone else. I have found it to be true that you may never know how much of an impact you may have on someone if you are not willing to help others.

Remain educated—Martin Luther King reminds us that, "The function of education is to teach one to think intensively and to think critically. Intelligence plus character—that is the goal of true education." Men should take the time to read books, research myths AND facts for the truth, discuss with others what has been learned, and put their thoughts in writing to help the next generation.

TROPHIES

What "Making It Look Easy" Means and Why It Is Important as Men

By Jamine C. Ifedi, MBA

Drake may have said it best in his 2014 smash hit "Trophies." "I'm just tryna stay alive and take care of my people. And they don't have no award for that... ain't no envelopes to open. I just do it 'cause I'm 'supposed to." In a day and age where you can easily upload on social media either true or false accolades about yourself to receive instant gratifications from the world, it is important for us to remind ourselves as men where our identity lies.

Manhood is not about the trophies or the recognition. The truth is, men that are consistently "handling their business," i.e. protecting and providing, instilling the fear of the Lord, and faithfully leading their family to their purpose, will never receive their due recognition. That's okay because you are not responsible to the world. It is not your job to love, clothe, and feed everyone on Facebook or Twitter. Conversely, it is not the job of everyone in your life to love and support you.

It has become increasingly important that we actively guard our time and attention. We must resist the urge to spend too much time and attention on the opinion of people on social media—or frankly anyone—whose success or failure is not directly tied to our own. Instead, we should redirect that time and attention to reinvest back into our family and close friends.

If not for the recognition, then what should be our driving force as men? The answer is simple, yet takes a lifetime for us to truly answer—it is our PURPOSE. Your purpose is the central motivating aim of your life; the reason you get up in the morning. Purpose has the potential to shape your goals, guide your life decisions, influence behaviors, provide a sense of direction, and ultimately create a source of meaning for your life. When everything you do is rooted in your purpose, you live with a destination in mind. When trials and tribulations come your way, you may get knocked down, but you always get back up because you know your mission has not yet been fulfilled.

Finding one's purpose and leading souls to Christ are the only two reasons we are sent to Earth. Everyone is born with a seed in them that has the potential to one day blossom into a forest of opportunity. In short, a successful life is to find our purpose and live it out in a way that honors and uplifts the Lord's name. This is why as men we *must not* be complacent, or seek trophies from the world, or simply seek employment, or even search for love. We *must* seek His Kingdom first.

Matthew 6:33 says, "But seek first God's Kingdom, and His righteousness; and all these things will be given to you as well." Many of us believe that seeking the Lord's kingdom means going to church often, paying a tithe, and following rules; but that, simply, is not enough. We were sent to this Earth to dominate it for His glory! We were sent here to bring Heaven's Kingdom down to Earth.

Each of us has been assigned a purpose, a task, something that you are responsible to fulfill before He calls you back up to Him. Have you figured out what your purpose is? If not, don't despair. I will let you in on a secret…most people die before they even realize they were assigned a purpose to fulfill. If you're able to see or hear these words, you still have a chance to figure it out. There is no age limit, height requirement, or financial mandate necessary. These seeds that have been planted into us are each unique. No two people have the same exact purpose. We can help each other achieve our purposes (a term known as a *destiny helper*), but there is a sense of ownership that you alone must accept for your life.

How I Make It Look Easy

I am less than a year away from my third collegiate graduation, to God be all the glory! I will receive my Doctor of Dental Surgery (DDS) from University of North Carolina at Chapel Hill to become a licensed dentist. This will be the culmination of my ten-year college career. As that day draws nearer, I often reflect on all the sleepless nights that have led to this moment.

A longtime friend Wilford Thomas once uttered the wise words, "The best problems are the problems that aren't yours." The truth is, outside of my family and small group of friends, not many people care about how many sleepless nights and missed life events it cost me to become a doctor. I have learned to accept this fact. I did not commit my life to healing and creating smiles for the recognition.

When patients come to me in distress or severe pain, all they care about is, "Can you deliver on your oath to provide superior dental care now that I need it?" The #1 question I receive is "How long will this procedure take?" Patients never ask "How long did you study to pass the competency for this procedure?"

As men it is important to reassess the source of our motivation. We must ask ourselves the important questions. What are the important questions you need to ask yourself? Here's a quick exercise to become more familiar with them.

Take out a sheet of paper, and number the page 1 through 4. Leave a few lines between each number so you can answer the following questions with as much detail as you can.

1. "What is my purpose?"
2. "Who am I working for?"
3. "What am I working for?"
4. "As the leader of my family, am I making the best use of my time to equip myself with the knowledge necessary to effectively and knowledgeably lead?"

Each question requires careful thought and deep introspection. The more you ask yourself these questions, the clearer your life becomes, and the more effective you will become at helping the rest of your family find their purpose and lead a successful life.

How You Can Make It Look Easy

"Like a tree bearing fruit, the world doesn't need you. The world only wants the fruit that you are carrying."
—**Dr. Myles Munroe**

Think back to the last time you ate an apple or an orange. Did you ever stop to think about how long that tree had to be planted and grow before it produced its first delectable fruit that you enjoy? In the same manner, people never stop to think about all your trials and tribulations that contributed to the man that you have become. It took one of the greatest players of all time, LeBron James, eight full seasons before he won his first championship. Most careers do not last eight years. Have you ever once stopped to think, "How many practice shots did it take LeBron James before he won that first championship?" Probably not.

As consumers we only bother ourselves with the product, the fruit, the service, or the gift someone has to offer. It's not our fault. It's human nature. At the end of LeBron's career, people won't remember the eight years of strife he suffered through in the beginning of his career. All they will care about is how he won three NBA

Finals (to date) and went to eight consecutive NBA Finals from 2011-2018. So, think for a moment…are you in the eighth season of your life? Like LeBron, are you still hunting for your first championship? What goals are you working on right now? What goals will you one day point to and proudly state, "This is the culmination of my life's work"?

For many reading this story, you are on a precipice of something great! I know this feeling all too well. It is hard to explain to others that may have never shared this weight. It is like you know something is coming, but you can't put it into words. You feel something knocking at the door, but you don't know what is on the other side.

Success is getting closer and closer, but you have come so close before in the past without attaining it. So now you're conditioned to be hesitant about allowing yourself to become completely invested. This is the moment when men stand up, and you seize your success. It will not just come to you.

This moment is when you tap into the deepest and truest essence of your manhood. This is when you burn the ships and completely, fully, and wholeheartedly push forward. You must ignore the socially programmed desires for acknowledgement to pre-maturely celebrate before the job is done. LeBron could have celebrated making it to his first NBA Finals and been content. Instead, he doubled down and locked in, refusing to settle for anything less than the goal he originally set.

Your mini-successes are only stepping stones, not the destination. Never forget that! Get back in the gym and keep putting shots up because your real success is on the other side of that door—what the Lord has planned for you. Your destiny is on the other side of that door. Your legacy is on the other side of that door. The air you need to breathe is on the other side of that door. Fight with everything you have and kick that door in! Take your championship by force because it was yours before you were created, and it's just waiting on you to claim it.

T.E.A.M. Manhood Golden Standard: There is no age limit, height requirement, or financial mandate necessary. These seeds that have been planted into us are each unique. No two people have the same exact purpose. We can help each other achieve our purposes (a term known as a *destiny helper*), but there is a sense of ownership that you alone must accept for your life. Your mini-successes are only stepping stones, not the destination. Never forget that! Get back in the gym and keep putting shots up because your real success is on the other side of that door—what the Lord has planned for you. Your destiny is on the other side of that door. Your legacy is on the other side of that door. The air you need to breathe is on the other side of that door. Fight with everything you have and kick that door in! Take your championship by force because it was yours before you were created, and it's just waiting on you to claim it.

MEN OF T.E.A.M.

By Casey C. Ifedi

The key to manhood is work. Work is the first command God gave to man.

Genesis 2:15 says, "The LORD God took the man and put him in the Garden of Eden to work it and take care of it." The word *work* has four meanings: 1. to become, 2. to manifest, 3. to fulfill, 4. to reveal. Your work is your gift. Work is not something that is retired from. A man's worth is found in his work, not from a woman. The greatest danger of man and manhood is ignorance of self and a lack of self-image. Character and integrity is the bedrock of all true leaders. My character and integrity was revealed my sophomore year in college. T.E.A.M. (Talented, Empowered, Aspired, Men) was created to inspire, encourage, and propel men and their family community.

Character and integrity of men compliment each other, but each has their own specific purpose. There are five distinct characteristics that make up a man of T.E.A.M. The first character trait of a T.E.A.M. man is *divine dominion*. A male in God's presence qualifies the male. The next character trait for a man is *to work*. A man must be able to manage their priorities. Before a man is able to properly love a woman, it is absolutely paramount he finds his work first. The third character trait that must be present is *cultivation*. The male is created to make everything around him better. He is to maximize every opportunity while being fruitful. Men must be able to create and cultivate opportunities, projects, and people. The ideal woman is out there, but it is up to the man to cultivate and bring out the very best from his woman. The fourth character trait is the ability *to protect and provide*. Some people may try to separate these two traits, but one is unable to protect if he is unable to provide. Men are biologically larger in composition and body mass in order to protect the woman. The last character trait of a man of T.E.A.M. is the ability *to teach truth, knowledge, and direction*. The man is the foundation of civilization. This is why it is important that men educate themselves and develop and exercise these traits daily.

Integrity is defined as being whole and undivided. Principle is constant and never changing. In other words, principles create laws that must be followed in order to achieve a desired outcome. The principle of integrity is what makes a male a man. Men of integrity are whole and complete in the same way God is one and undivided. A man of integrity is one. One of the fundamental traits of men is the ability to be complete and whole. Men are able to be integral and impose self-discipline. The concept of integrity is grounded in principal. A man of integrity is committed to his values and character. Character is prioritized over all other traits. Many politicians believe that their private life is different from their public service. When a man has character and integrity, both private and public life are the same. A person with integrity does not have to speak or teach about life. The ultimate example is a life lived.

The only way to test character is through temptation. Temptation is not a negative event. Temptation is to temper or to test for weakness. When a house is built, one will never truly know how strong the foundation is until it is tested through different weather conditions that reveal the true content of the structure. There are three matters that will reveal a man's true integrity and character—power, money, and access to sex. Until a man has proven he can handle the temptation from all three areas, a man's character is not complete.

The greatest danger of man and manhood is ignorance of self and a lack of self-image. Character and integrity is the bedrock of all true leaders.

My character and integrity was revealed my sophomore year in college. During this time we created The T.E.A.M. vs. The Squad Mentor and Mentee program. We were set to meet Saturday mornings at 3rd Street Community Center in Greenville, NC. During our time there, we were informed that Pitt County was the number one county in the United States for fatherless homes. This news deeply disturbed me. The T.E.A.M. was an organization full of educated, talented, and willing men in a city full of lost men with no clear vision and image of true manhood. We decided to commit to the Saturday program.

Every first and second Saturday we spent time volunteering at the Community Center with the youth. Most of the men were able to attend those Saturdays; but as time progressed, less and less members would show up to the program. I planned an emergency meeting to understand why so many men in our organization stopped showing up for our community program.

During the meeting, I noticed one common theme that continually reappeared. Many members struggled with volunteering and waking up Saturday morning for three main reasons. The first was many of the guys found it difficult to sacrifice their Friday nights, which allowed them to receive enough rest for the following day.

The second reason was a lack of value and discipline. When we first started the program, it was easy for members to follow the status quo. The level of excitement and energy was high, and The T.E.A.M. vs. The Squad Program required little effort because the e-board took responsibility to arrange and organize the entire program for the general body. The idea was that once we created the platform for service and community, the rest of the members would be able to step up and run the program completely. What we found was that some of the members never valued the program to begin with. They may have enjoyed the program—some even expressed their desire to continue the program—but they lacked the discipline to see the project through. The last reason was that some of the members were not integral. What was projected or started by the brothers was not consistent with their actions. What I noticed about all of the men that were consistent and present for The T.E.A.M. vs. The Squad morning mentorship program was that each man possessed a level of character and integrity. It requires character to see anything in life through to fruition. What happens for many people is that they see the ultimate finished product or image of a goal and dream. Where many miss the mark is that they either underestimate or do not correctly predict the amount of effort that will be needed to complete the action. Character will be needed to continue even when the feelings and emotions behind the decisions begin to dwindle.

Each Saturday there were a select few of our members that would show up. We met at the Community Center at 9am sharp. The first item of each visit was to tutor the children and go over at least one life lesson before hitting the field for a discussion and to play football. I noticed that The Squad followed us and wanted to huddle up with us. Up until this point, I still viewed myself as adolescence. I have always been mature, but this moment felt different. It was as if I was the general, a coach of sorts. The guys wanted to hear what I had to say. It felt like they respected me not because of what I said, but how I lived my life. It is The T.E.A.M.'s character and integrity of manhood that marked a clear difference between my adolescent life and manhood.

As we stood huddled on the field, I started to explain the difference between boys and men. "Both men and boys are born male, but one becomes the other. It is important for each male to have visions and dreams for his life. A man's work defines his masculinity. The male's purpose is linked to his work." As I made these statements, I could visually see the confusion. Each young man in the huddle was excited to hear more. I said, "Regardless of race, religion, culture, or age, two qualifiers create manhood. The foundation of manhood is work and purpose. Nothing is more important in the life of a man than his life's work and purpose. A man's work is the vehicle to find and fulfill his purpose. That's enough for now; let's get this game started! The T.E.A.M. vs. The Squad…who will win?"

After the end of the game, we gathered everyone together to go over everything.

"I would like to thank you all for coming out early on a Saturday morning. Today I noticed something that will stick with me. The Squad played hard and never gave up. You guys were able to delegate your individual talents to maximize your opportunity. It was almost as if you all knew where your deficits were and positioned yourselves in order to take advantage of the game.

"The way you all played today is similar to how life is to be lived. The best part is that everything needed is within. There is no need to search outside of self when tapping into your purpose. Gifts and talents are manifested through work, which help create purpose. Purpose fulfilled is the ultimate destination of manhood. Manhood is therefore defined by a man's work and his ability to accomplish purpose. The road to purpose is not a straight line. Rather, it is a journey of peaks and valleys. During the journey of life, there are many obstacles that work to derail a man's destiny. Media, society, priorities, agendas, and fear are at the mountain peaks of distractions."

I took a step back and looked straight at all of the members of The T.E.A.M. and The Squad and explained all of the factors that affect manhood in the 21st century. "We are up against a lot, brothers. But one of our biggest weapons at our disposal is our T.E.A.M. and our network of Men. We are The Men of T.E.A.M. I believe in you, and together we will accomplish our God given purpose." I looked and smiled at our community of men, and they all collectively said, "The T.E.A.M.—Character and Integrity of Manhood!"

Will you rise up? Join the winning T.E.A.M. Character and integrity is the bedrock of all true leaders. T.E.A.M. inspires, encourages, and propels men and their family community. We will work and fulfill our purpose—we will be men that lead positive change in our generation. We are the standard of manhood in the 21st century.

T.E.A.M. Manhood Golden Standard: Both men and boys are born male, but one becomes the other. It is important for each male to have visions and dreams for his life. A man's work defines his masculinity. The male's purpose is linked to his work. The foundation of manhood is work and purpose. Nothing is more important in the life of a man than his life's work and purpose. A man's work is the vehicle to find and fulfill his purpose.

ABOUT THE AUTHORS

Casey Chinedu Ifedi

Casey Chinedu Ifedi is a licensed Realtor and Property Manager in the state of North Carolina. From student housing, real estate consultation and real estate investing; both professionally and personally, Mr. Ifedi works with clients to create a practical and holistic real estate strategy. Mr. Ifedi brings a team of lenders, credit experts, and qualified professionals that work together to bring the client the highest quality in service and representation.

As a graduate and former student-housing advisor at East Carolina University, Mr. Ifedi worked to improve the student housing experience. While a student at ECU, Casey was able to create The T.E.A.M., which created open dialogue between students and faculty in improving and enhancing the on-campus experience. Through this opportunity Casey has been able to transition his time on campus to a full-time real estate career focused on maximizing the management, profit margins, and overall well-being of every client.

Email: Casey_3010@yahoo.com
Number:704-301-8399
IG: C.Ifedi | Facebook: GenChinedu

Chris Graham

Chris Graham is an entrepreneur who adapted the belief that he has a responsibility to continually grow himself personally and professionally, to help as many people as possible. To practice this principle, he challenged himself to start a second business, Holistic Coaching 4F Group, founded in 2019. That year he also chose to treat couples predominantly. Since that time, he has accumulated thousands of hours delivering counseling to intimate partners seeking healing from various relationship issues. Through this journey, Chris used the experiences and training as a Life Coach to author my first book, *T.E.A.M. Character & Integrity of Manhood.*

Chris Graham is the owner of T.E.A.M. Talk Productions and FF- Foundation Inc, a nonprofit focusing on boys and girls' trajectory from 8-18 years old.

www.facebook.com/groups/21stcenturyman

www.ingramcontent.com/pod-product-compliance
Lightning Source LLC
Chambersburg PA
CBHW071222160426
43196CB00012B/2380